Isn't God Worth the Wait?
Erase and Replace

Latina C. Campbell

Copyright © 2018 Latina C. Campbell

All rights reserved. No part of this book may be reproduced in any form or by any electronic or mechanical means, including information storage and retrieval systems, without permission in writing from the publisher, except by reviewers, who may quote brief passages in a review.

ISBN: 9781732381155
Library of Congress Control Number: 2018907508
Printed in the United States of America

Story Corner Publishing LLC.
6024 Churchland Blvd. Suite 10
Portsmouth, VA 23703
Storycornerpublishing@yahoo.com

Dedication

I dedicate this book first and foremost back to God, because without Him I would not have had the courage to even write this story. We overcome obstacles by others testimonies, so I pray that you are encouraged after reading this story. I also dedicate this book to all of the people struggling with a void in their lives. I pray this book finds you and brings you comfort and strength.
All Glory Be To God!!

Contents

Chapter 1 This Can't Be Life..1

Chapter 2 The Business Deal..7

Chapter 3 Torn..11

Chapter 4 It's On The Way..14

Chapter 5 Life Changes In A Blink Of An Eye...................................21

Chapter 6 Her New Apartment...30

Chapter 7 The Downward Spiral..37

Chapter 8 Daddy's Gone...43

Chapter 9 That Night..48

Prayer

Thank you God for all that you have done in my life. Thank you God for forgiving me for all that I have sin each and every day. Without you I am nothing, but with you I am something. Thank you for never leaving me. Thank you for waiting on me to step into your presence. Thank you for loving me when I did not even love myself. Thank you for your mercy, grace, blessings, and favor. Please continue to shower me with your knowledge, courage, wisdom, strength, and understanding. I should've died a long time ago, but you seen it fit to cover and protect me. I owe everything to you God! I will serve you forever. Without you this book or testimony of life would be possible. God please touch the heart, mind, and soul of every reader. God please transform their lives to look like you. Please bless them, supply all of their needs, and fulfill their hearts desires. Also, help them to realize that You are the void filler and draw them closer to you in the Mighty Name of Jesus Christ, Amen.

Love Notes

The importance of LOVE is so great. No matter who you are, you need love.

The bible declares *"Above all, love each other deeply, because love covers over a multitude of sins." (1Peter 4:8 NIV version).* What does that mean?? When you love someone there will be certain things you do, and certain things you don't do. Therefore, if you love someone, sin (evil, mean, & hatful things), will Not take place. A lot of sinful thoughts, actions, & words will pass you by if you continue to love no matter what. Of course love is an action word, so your actions should always display love. When you love someone, you have to love them despite their flaws and sins. Many of us say we love, but do not even know what love really is.

What is Love?

The bible declares "Love is patience, love is kind. It does not envy, it does not boast, it is not proud. It does not dishonor others, it is not self-seeking, it is not easily angered, it keeps no record of wrongs. Love does not delight in evil but rejoices with the truth. It always protects, always trusts, always hopes, always perseveres. Love never fails." (1Corinthians 13:4-8 NIV version).

The bible also declares *"And now these three remain: faith, hope, and love. But the greatest of these is Love." (1Corinthians 13:13 NIV version).*

So let's love ourselves and each other God's way, and not the way the world taught us to love.

Chapter. 1
This Can't Be Life

There was this girl that was born into a world that had most of the cards stacked against her. She lived in the inner city where drugs was sold on every corner. There were at least ten liquor stores in every neighborhood, and prostitution was going on so freely that everyone accepted it as the norm.

Camden, New Jersey was where she called home. Growing up, she thought the world looked all the same. She didn't realize there was so much more to explore then the streets of Camden. Every day she made up her own reality because she hated how her life was going. Being a teenager, there was not much she could do to change her situation so she just hoped and dreamed it would magically change one day.

She loved princess movies because she always put herself in their shoes hoping her Prince Charming would rescue her from the actual reality she lived in. Even though she seen that there was not much she could do to change her life at the moment, she always had a feeling that there just had to be more out there.

The summer of 2000, she had graduated from the 8th grade and was about fourteen years old. She was so excited to finally be on her way to high school! This high school had the most school spirit in the city, Camden High School.

It was always in her mind that after high school she would move out because she was considered an adult. Just maybe her life would change for the better and she would have a greater chance at finding Prince Charming to live happily ever after with; The End. So the task of completing high school was upon her and hanging over her head like a ton of bricks.

She was always a smart student but as she got older more and more distractions came her way. Now don't get me wrong, she has had it up to her neck with distractions! For example, the electric would be off every other month and she had to use candles to do her homework. The gas would be off as well which meant there would be no heat or hot water! Therefore, she had to wear her coat to bed in the winter and wash up in cold water. She had to wash clothes in the bath tub because they could not afford to take the clothes to laundry mat. She bathed in the bathroom sink or a bowl because the flooring in the bathroom was too weak to hold any real weight in it. Limited food today then none tomorrow, so distractions were everywhere. You name it and she had been through it! It was like living in a third world country right in the U.S.

The house was definitely not up to proper living standards at all. When she would lay in her bed she could see the stars, moon, and everything else in the sky because there were holes in the roof. Literally holes in the roof! When it rained, it poured right on her bed! She also knew what the breeze felt like outside before she even got out there because there were huge spaces in the brinks of her room walls. There was even a tree that grew up the side of the house, helping the bricks to continue to space out. Oh and let's not forget about the things that lived in the tree that found their way into her room, like the birds and the bees. The bees definitely made their presence known with the painful bee strings in the middle of the night. She definitely had every right to be distracted, but she had to fight through it all! No room for delay and she definitely could not turn back now! She thought life could not get any harder until one afternoon her mother announced she was leaving her father!

She was the oldest of five and this news hit everyone hard, but it hit her the hardest because she was *daddy's little girl*. She was upset, confused, and angry at her mother! Apparently, her mother was sick of the way everything was going. So her mother decided to just pack up and take her and her siblings away. With no money, no job, and no support from family or friends, her mother had no choice but to turn to the nearest shelter.

She resented her mother for leaving her father behind. Daddy's little girl could not picture life without him always there. She did not want to be like other single parent families, but off to the shelter they went.

She hated everything about the shelter! It felt like she was in prison. There were rules and regulations for everything!

Rules like:

*Wake up and go to sleep at a certain time.

*Eat and shower at a certain time.

*List of chores.

*Banned from building between morning and noon.

*Set curfew at night!

The food was horrible! It was the same food hospital patients ate. It was always freezing cold in the shelter and the beds felt like she was sleeping on the floor because they were so hard. She was sure this was the bottom of life and she thought about giving up each and every day!

The only thing that kept her motivated to move forward was her siblings. She was the oldest and had always been there for them through it all. She felt like she had to be their protector. She knew if she gave up at this point her siblings would be lost forever, so she had to hang in there.

But as the days went on, she could see a change in her mother. A change that she never thought she would see. Her mother had been a substance abuser for many years of her life, but this drastic step helped her mother to see that she COULD live without the substance that controlled her life for so long. No more did her mother feel the need to use drugs to cope with the stressors of life. Her mother decided to take back the control of her life and she quit the drug! Yes, her mother quit using drugs and never looked back!

She became so proud of her mother and forgot that she was even upset with her as the days went on. Her mother began to show her a different side that she never saw before. She saw dedication and courage! She had always prayed her mother would one day stop using drugs and that the family would come together like never before. She got her prayers answered, glory to God, but still didn't understand why life still looked so bad. Since she could not give up, she had to push even harder in high school because she had to graduate before she could move out and start her own life. She hoped her siblings took note of all that she was doing and started goals for themselves as well.

After almost a year of living in the shelter, her mother found a house that they could afford to rent. Her and her siblings were so filled with joy that they did not even care where it was. Just as long as it was NOT the shelter!!

Not only was she about to be set free from the jail, meaning the "shelter", but her mother had been "clean" or free of drug use since the first day they went to the shelter! She could not believe that

God heard her prayers and answered them! Everything was going great! She no longer resented her mother because she started to understand that every step of the process was necessary in order to create this "better life."

Chapter. 2
The Business Deal

As the years flew, she was now an eleventh grader. Almost an adult, she could see what color her own kitchen would be. She could also see what kind of towels she would have in her bathroom and most importantly it would be her own! There was space and freedom to do whatever she wanted to do and she would be in control of her own destiny. She had goals. She wanted to move into her own place, get her diving license, get a job, get a car, then go to college or the military, and start a career. She wanted to be an FBI agent most of all! She remembered as a kid watching the TV show *XFiles* and wanting to be just like the star characters that were FBI agents.

Of course if Prince Charming came her way, she would fit him in to settle down with her and get married and have some kids. She had her whole life all planned out. No one could change her mind and she was more determined than ever. She could now see the light at the end of the tunnel, meaning this chapter of her life was finally coming to an end and a new one was about to begin. A few months into the school year and everything was going great. All she could think about was marching down the aisle as they called her name to receive her diploma in her hand.

She was focused. That is, until she met this guy. This guy was handsome, and had an athletic body, clear skin, and a great smile. He was charming, dressed well, and always knew just what to say. She did not think she would meet Prince Charming this fast! But she sure was not trying to push him away just in case he was the man of her dreams.

She fell for this guy instantly. It was almost like he had a spell on her. She never wanted to leave his side, but she knew that wasn't realistic especially if she was going to carry out the rest of her goals and dreams on her list of things to accomplish. This guy kept her interest and she wanted to know more and more about him each and every day. She was falling in love with everything about him and to top it all off, he always smelled sooooooo wonderful! His scent was intoxicating and made her weak at the knees. She could smell him in her sleep! How was this possible?? She never understood it, but it was so.

She decided to give him a chance and make him hers. Although she was young, she knew about making the guy wait for anything sexual so that she could get to know him first. She did not want to regret rushing into things. She made him wait ninety days starting on the day they exchanged titles as boyfriend/ girlfriend.

She thought of the dating world as a business. Relationships should begin just as you would start a job. First, you would fill out your job application and submit it. In the dating world, that first five minute conversation while you're storing their phone number would be the application process. Next, the employer goes through the pile of applications to see who they want to call back which would be equivalent to who stood out in your mind the most and you wanted to give them a call. Then after the employer calls the small group of people, they set up interviews to see who gets hired. In the dating world, choosing who gets to go out on a date with you is the interview.

After the interview the employer determines who was the most qualified and then they are hired, which would be equivalent to deciding who you would like to get to know further after the round of dates. Lastly, the person who is hired is on a ninety day probation period to see if they measure up to everything they said they could and would do in their interview and only after the probation period will they earn all of their benefits. In the dating world, the person you chose to get to know further passed the test period and they get whatever benefits you choose to reward them with. (Note: It is Best & Recommended to Wait until Marriage to have sex). So if this guy made it through the hiring process and pass the probation period she would reward him with his benefit package. But if he did not make it through the probation period, he would be fired!!

This guy would be her first boyfriend, if he passed and would be the first person to go through the ninety day process. Their chemistry was magical and he actually was dedicated to passing the test to be with her forever. They grew so deeply in love during the trial period that the ninety days seemed to take eternity to arrive, but they waited. Finally, ninety days had arrived and he passed!! He made it through the hiring process and successfully passed his probationary period. Now she wanted to reward him with his benefit package, the benefits of her body and soul.

She gave him every piece of her and did not want anyone else at this point. She only had eyes for him. She just knew he was "the one" and she started picturing him in the life that she had been planning all these years. She finally was able to put a face to the Prince Charming of her dreams and the wait to find him was over.

Chapter. 3
Torn

A year into their relationship and so many things had happened. Where to start? It truly felt like she was on a rollercoaster ride. So many twist and turns that she found herself confused, alone, and depressed. No more did she feel the butterflies of love. Yes, she still loved him deeply, but she could feel that something just was not right. After the "fairytale" love had passed, she started to see things differently. How did she feel alone while she was in a relationship?? Where was the guy she fell in love with? Why did she feel depressed? Doesn't love bring joy and not pain?

She realized there was still a void in her love life that was not being fulfilled. She started to question if he was "the one." Everything seemed out of place and she did not feel that same spark anymore. He felt her drifting away and decided to try to rekindle their love by popping the big question. He proposed to her! She should've been excited now, right? There was still something missing, and she knew getting married was not it. Again, she loved him very much, but she definitely did not want to rush into marriage. So she decided that they were too young and she needed more time to make sure this was the right choice. She did not believe in divorce, so whoever she married would be her last! She did not want to make a mistake.

Soon after the proposal, she found out he was cheating on her and that all of the things she felt had started making sense. She was devastated!!! Her heart was broken into a thousand pieces. All of those excuses of why he could not visit her, the unanswered phone calls/ text, and the lies all started to add up now. She did not know what to do, but of course she had to leave him. So she left.

Torn, broken, and vulnerable she was put back into the mental place she was in when her mother left her father. Another man gone from her life that she truly loved! That void came back to the surface and all those feelings ran crazy through her mind. She felt like that helpless little girl that had no control over her life again. She had to fill the void fast before it drove her off of a bridge. She did not know how to cope with these feelings, so what better way but to *"erase and replace."* She thought she would erase the memories of the hurt and loss then replace the person who did these things to her with someone or something else.

The cycle of *"erase and replace"* had begun. Although she was trying to erase her ex-boyfriend out of her mind, she still loved him. She knew she had to move on with the plan to eventually replace him, so she did.

Chapter. 4
It's On The Way

There was this guy at school who came along and started showering her with attention. He seemed to really like her, but she did not feel the same way about him. He just would not leave her alone, so she figured he would have been an easy substitute as the person to replace her ex-boyfriend. She did think he was cute, but he was too arrogant and into himself and she hated that about him.

After the brokenness and vulnerability took over her mind, she put herself in a compromising position and she slept with the guy from school, unprotected! She threw the ninety day process out of the window and thought that sex would fix her void because she was hurt by her ex-boyfriend when he had sex with someone else. She thought sex was what kept a guy interested since her ex compromised their relationship for it.

After having a one night stand with the guy from school, she became pregnant and she knew she was not ready for a baby. Her life as she knew it would be over! So without really processing all options, she immediately decided to get an abortion. She was off to *"erase and replace"* again! She kept this secret just between her and her best friend. She did not know how to tell her mother until she found out she needed a ride to the clinic along with her mother's consent because she was not eighteen years old yet. She had to tell her mother if she wanted to go forward with the plan. Nervous and afraid, she told her mother the news. Her mother was disappointed, but surprised that she arranged everything on her own and this was something she was sure about.

Her life changed in a blink of an eye and she had to erase memories just as fast so they did not settle in her mind. One moment changed her life forever. She wished she could turn back the hands of time to get the chance to make a better choice, like never sleeping with the guy from school in the first place, but she couldn't. She just had to move forward from here.

She let the hurt from her ex-boyfriend get the best of her and allowed it to alter her way of thinking. Operating out of emotion made her do things she knew was wrong, like having unprotected sex with someone who did not even deserve her. He was not even someone she wanted to marry and be with forever. She did a long term gesture with a temporary person. She made a mistake! She got the abortion right away. It was the best choice for her in her mind at the time because of the circumstances. She asked God for forgiveness because she knew it was morally wrong and she felt bad about it. She also knew it was damaging to her body. So she was thankful that the God she acknowledged is a forgiving God that keeps no record of the wrongs that she brought to Him. She had a speedy recovery and she was grateful about it.

Days went by and she started feeling depressed and alone even more. For some reason, she felt another loss took place in her life after the abortion even though she was clear in her decision. She tried to figure this feeling out, but she kept coming up blank and more depressed. The empty place started making her second guess the choice she made. Should she have kept the baby? Life would not have made sense if she did! But why is life not making any sense now? She was already battling with rejection and abandonment, now her loneliness was speaking to her. She had to shake it off! She missed her ex-boyfriend like crazy during this time. Maybe that was the loneliness speaking to her too. Yes, he hurt her, but she still missed the connection they had in the beginning and all the good moments they spent together. It felt like years since she left him, but it was only weeks.

After weeks of him apologizing to her and making efforts to fix their relationship, she gave in. She still loved him so it was hard for her to stay away for good. She knew she had to tell him what had happen during the time they were broken up because she did not feel right holding it in for some reason. She could have buried it in her mind because he would've never found out, but she just felt like he should know since she still planned on being with him forever. Of course it was really none of his business since they were broken up at the time, but she did not want any secrets between them, even though he held things from her. She really felt bad because her first child was not with him and having children together was all he talked about the whole relationship.

They met up and she shared all that had happened. He was hurt, but decided to move past it. He loved her too much to let that situation come between them.

Another year had gone by and she was now in the twelfth grade!!! Still many trials and tribulations in their relationship, but they worked through them. He wanted a family now and was not trying to take "No" for an answer. She was only a couple months into the school year and knew her education was first, no matter what.

He proposed again and she pushed it off again. She still needed a little more time. A few weeks later her mother made the announcement that they would be moving very soon. The contractors just had to put the finishing touches on the brand new home that her mother had worked very hard to get. That moment should have been a time to celebrate, but instead all she could think of was the space that was about to come between her and her boyfriend. She would have to leave her boyfriend on the other side of town. With no car, seeing each other would be a hassle. She thought she was losing him after she had finally taken him back. She did not want to leave him so she sat and thought of ways that they could be attached and never apart! She came up blank and frustrated!

Then she had this bright idea one day of having his baby since he kept asking her. She felt that would have kept him attached to her since they would be having the baby together and this is what he always wanted from her. Of course he wanted marriage too, but she felt like that could wait a little while longer since he said he loved her. She presented the baby idea to him and before she could even finish the sentence he was ready to give her body a test run.

He immediately took her to his house and undressed her. He had his way with her and it was an experience they never felt before. They had the best sex they ever had!! Two weeks flew by and she took a pregnancy test out of curiosity and she was pregnant! The first time he gave her everything during their love making process and she became pregnant. Yikes!!

She told him the news and he was super excited! They both just knew that this baby would make them whole as a family and keep them together no matter what. Months later she moved into the new house with her mother and he visited her every day. He was the greatest *dad to be* during her pregnancy! He was there every step of the way. She did not share this news with her parents yet because she did not know how to tell them. She knew they would not be pleased because they wanted better for her and wanted her to finish school above all things. They definitely did not want her to become a statistic. A statistic is a fact or piece of data from a study of large quantity of numerical data. In other words, falling into the category society expects you to fall in depending on your race, age, and gender. Statistics of a black teenage girl getting pregnant, dropping out of school, and ending up in the welfare system was at an all time high in poor cities. Statistics show motherhood erases hopes and dreams. Mothers even end up giving up on independent, freedom, and control of their own lives. But she was determined not to fall into the statistic category!

Her family did not want anything getting between her and her goals. She knew that they just wanted the best for her because they loved her, so she waited to tell them the news of her being pregnant. She could not change the fact that she was pregnant now, nor did she want to. A few months had gone by and her due date was around the corner, so she could not hold the secret from her parents any longer. It was time to face them and come clean. She told her boyfriend what she had to do and he was scared. She had her boyfriend come over so they could tell her mother together first. Her mother did not take it well at all. Her mother had a million questions that she did not prepare for so she could have answers ready to give. Questions like, "What house are you guys moving to? What jobs are you guys getting? How are you going to support this baby? What are you guys future plans? Are you finishing high school and going to college? And when are you guys getting married?"

She did not know all the answers to her mother's questions, but she did know she was still going forward with her list of goals despite her being pregnant. She wanted to prove the statistics wrong! She also knew she would get married one day because she planned to be with her boyfriend forever. It was a shock to hear her mother ask her about getting married when her mother was the same one that told her to wait on getting married! Her mother felt she was too young when she brought the idea to her the first time, but now her mother was the one rushing her to get married because of the baby on the way. She was only a year older since first proposal, so how is she old enough to get married now? Her mother was upset, but she dropped the conversation and told her to get a plan fast because there is no more time to waste. A few days went by and it was time to tell her dad.

Telling daddy was not going to be an easy task because she was daddy's little girl and no one was good enough for his daughter in his eyes! Her mother gave her a ride to her dad's house. She was torn with emotion because she was excited to see her dad and nervous to tell him the news! They pulled up to his house and he met her at the door. To her surprise her mother already told him the news of her pregnancy! Her dad asked her was it true and when she said, "yes", the look on her dads face was priceless. He looked at her in disappointment. It was a look she never seen on his face before. It crushed her heart to see her dad looking so let down.

Her dad had high hopes for her and he just knew that a baby would set her back like so many others he had witnessed. He asked her the same questions her mother asked her. All she knew was that her goals would be accomplished! She did not know how and when, but they were going to get done no matter what. From that day forward, all she could think about was the next level of her life that she had to take and fast! She was always goal minded. Creating goal after goal was not the issue, it was the timing.

Chapter. 5
Life Changes In A Blink Of An Eye

Today was the day she finally finished high school! It felt like it was taking forever to finish out the last couple months, but she made it! Eternity was a word she thought of every single day. She was about four months pregnant, but she didn't allow that to hold her back. Finishing high school was a big accomplishment for her. This was just one goal down and many more to conquer.

She started college during the fall semester right after high school and marked another goal off her list. She was about six months pregnant at this time, but she continued to push through. She was determined to be successful in the things she set out to do. She also got her driving license and a car around the same time, so she marked that off of her list as well. A couple months into her first college semester she gave birth to her beautiful baby girl on October 21, 2004. When she saw her baby for the first time her heart just melted! If she never felt or knew of love at first sight, this was it. She loved her more than life itself and she wanted to give her the world no matter what she had to do to accomplish that!!

All of her doubts, fears, brokenness, and heartaches melted away when she looked into her baby girl's eyes. She could gaze into her daughter's eyes and never get tired of doing it. She accomplished surviving the rollercoaster ride of pregnancy and brought new life into the world. Now she has entered the next phase of her life, getting through college then starting a career. In the meantime, she got a couple of jobs to bring in finances while she was in college. She started to realize how hard it was trying to juggle being in a relationship, a mom, a student, and working all at the same time! She began to feel weighed down and stressed out! She felt as if the whole world rested on her shoulders. She started to realize she spent more time running around getting her life in order that she felt alone again. She use to think a baby would bring them closer together, but now she see that it only drew them apart.

Where was the guy that wanted this family with her? Where was the guy that made her feel pressured about having his baby? Where was the guy that said he would be by her side fighting the storm with her no matter what, forever and always? He visited her less and less now that the baby was born. Where was he? She needed help! Doing everything alone was more stress and work. He did not have a job or go to school, so what was his excuse? Come to find out he was out doing what he did right before she broke up with him a while back, CHEATING! The town they lived in was so small that everyone knew everyone business, so it was not hard for her to get information. He was at it again! Let me say it again… He was out cheating while she was putting in work trying to be the best she could be for their new family.

At this time their daughter was about four months old and she called it quits for good! She felt like she could do bad all by herself. She did not need him at this point anyway because she already felt alone and was doing everything by herself. He was not bringing in finances to help support their family, nor was he spending any time with them, so he had to go. It was time for her to move out of her mother's house and she could not wait on him to get his life together. Time was running out!! She had an agenda with a ticking timer on it. She had hoped that her new life would have had him in it, but instead he had another agenda that was not to her liking.

It hurt her like hell being as though this was her first real relationship, first love, and child's father. The plan she thought would work out fail traumatically! She had to move on for the sake of her sanity and daughter's future. She invested so much time and energy! She really had her heart set on him being her future husband. What if she would've married him when he first asked? Would it have been the same outcome? She was stressed and depressed, but she was relieved that she did not marry him because he was not "the one." She thought a baby would keep them together and it didn't, so surely marriage would not have kept them together. If he was "the one," he would've been committed and willing to partner with her to create a better life for their family. She quickly learned it's all up to the person's commitment to the relationship and he had no commitment whatsoever! She was committed and he was not. He picked and chose when he wanted to be there and when he didn't. Relationships are a full time job plus overtime even when we are tired and just want to go home. There is no turn off and on switch. Either you are in it or you are not. It's that simple. She made her decision and didn't look back.

So much for her happily ever after!! Now she was a single mother trying to figure out life. If only her eyes would've been open to this before they had the baby. Oh well it's done now she thought. She couldn't turn back time, so there was no need to dwell on that. Back to the mindset and cycle of *"erase and replace"* she goes. She switched jobs and started working at this retail store that she hated!! She worked there for one day and was ready to quit, but she knew she needed money to take care of her daughter so she was stuck there for a while!

After the first week of working there the manager started showing interest in her. Personal interest in her! He was definitely NOT her type. She was lonely and broken all over again though. All she could think of was taking her mind off of her current situation, so she started flirting with him. In her mind it was just something to do, until he came out and shared how he really felt about her. She did not expect that, so she had to quickly let him know she was not interested in him that way. She didn't want to hurt someone else just because she was hurting. He seemed like he understood and she stopped flirting with him.

About a month went by and the store hired a few new employees. One of the employees looked like someone straight out of a magazine!! He was tall with abs for days. His body was built like he lived at a gym since birth! He had smooth skin like warm honey, hair like silk, smile as bright as the sun, and he always smelled sweet like candy. Yummy! She locked eyes with him once and was in love!!! In love again, that is! She just knew he would be hers no matter what. The butterflies were singing inside of her like she never heard before. Her heart skipped a beat every time she laid eyes on him. He was like no other guy she had seen before! He was sooooo beautiful!! Yes handsome, but the beauty that shined from him was as radiant as the sun rays at high noon!! She loved him and didn't even know him. She was Crazy in love and couldn't turn it off.

She let a few days go by as she kept her eyes on him to get a feel of who he was. She was so intrigued by him and began to worship him as a goddess in her sight. With him being a new employee, she could not wait to get to work each day! What made it even better was that they worked the same schedule. It was just meant to be. She started to enjoy being at work now, even though it was only because of him.

After about a week she finally started talking to him here and there with little flirtatious comments. Come to find out, he was just as interested in her as she was in him. He was checking her out too! He did not know how to approach her, so he was trying to come up with a plan. That was until she approached him first. They both were nervous to release their feelings and interest to one another, but they knew it had to be done or they would go insane!!! He asked her out on a date and from that point forward they fell so deep in love with each other that they couldn't breathe without each other.

They spent every moment together. Everyone hated seeing them together because they were so publicly affectionate with each other. She did not care though and neither did he. She did not think it was possible to love another guy deeper than she loved her first, but she did. They did all of the cute corny stuff together like wearing matching clothes, kissing 24/7, holding hands everywhere, switching name tags at work, etc… If you can think of it, they did it. Of course the manager that liked her first had a problem with all of this affection she was giving to someone else. He hated the fact that it was not him all glued to her. So he tried to find any little thing to break them up even if he had to fire one of them.

The manager started harassing them every day! A few weeks went by and the manager ended up getting forced to transfer to another store. They just watched how the tables turned and they did not even have to do anything. After a few months she left the job and went to work for another retail store that paid a little more. She hated that job too, but having her boyfriend on her mind helped her get through her work shifts day after day. They made sure they seen each other every day! It was like they would die if they were apart too long.

A couple months into their relationship he had a surprise for her. He always tried to do special things that he thought would bring a smile to her face. He showed up to her house and asked her to step outside. He turned his head to the side and there she seen it! Her name tattooed on his neck!!! She was lost for words and did not know how to respond!

She had mixed emotions. On one hand, she was flattered because he went through pain for her to feel special and it was a permanent gesture. But on the other hand, she was extra nervous and reality started to hit her all at once! Her void started to uncover itself. It started bringing up her old hurt and pain. She began to become afraid of the full commitment because she thought the same thing her ex did to her would happen all over again. The way she loved her new boyfriend was like no other, so if he hurt her it would destroy her! The reality was she rushed into another relationship solely because she was still emotionally broken by her ex-boyfriend. Was this guy truly the one to complete her "ready made" family? She had so many questions at this point. She did not think past the butterflies that she felt when she first laid eyes on him. Nor did she have a future plan for him in her mind. She only thought of plans for the moment. But clearly he wanted forever plans with her. She started to think of all of the forever plans she made with her ex that fell through and began to compare.

Did this guy really know what he was getting himself into? So many questions/concerns hit her at once that she just shut down and pushed him far away. She had never been this scared to react before. What should she do? It's almost like she was stuck with him now because her name was signed on his neck! Her mind just kept shifting back and forth between thought after thought. She wanted him to go, but she also wanted him to stay! She was torn in between the two emotions because she was not fully healed from the last hurt! She then realized that she was still broken over the last relationship and had not fully let go of the pain and trauma. She did not want to damage anyone else the way she got damaged, so she did what she did best, RUN!

She really did love him, but she just needed some more time. It was not just about her anymore either. She had a child to consider that she wanted the absolute best for, even if she had to sacrifice some things or people. Her love for her daughter overrode any other type of love, so she had to be sure he was the one to fill the gap. Nor did she want to invest her all again and get taken advantage of. She did not want to become heartbroken all over again, or have someone let her daughter down either.

She told him how she felt, but it did not go so well. He felt rejected, hurt, and thought there was someone else. He was not understanding of her feelings, so they split up. The fire love was over and she fell into a depression that she thought she would never recover from. The ending of this relationship felt indescribable. She ended the relationship because she was scared and wanted to make sure he was the best father figure for her daughter, but she was still madly in love with him. She did not understand anything that had happened, but she did understand the way she processed emotions from a situation that she did not want to deal with anymore, "erase and replace."

It was almost like she broke her own heart and then went out to find someone who did not even love or care about her to fix it. She moved on to another nameless guy that only wanted to use her body during his moments of boredom. She was okay with it because she did not want any commitments. She got tired of him after a while then *erased and replaced* him with someone who was hurt by his ex-girlfriend, so he was not looking for anything serious. He was still dealing with loss and pain as well. She knew she could not stay in this because she was dealing with her own baggage and did not have time for someone else's. Therefore, she cut him loose too.

Chapter 6
Her New Apartment

She had finished her second year of college and things started getting rough between her and her mother. They started arguing on the regular!! She knew it was past the time she had planned to move out, but she wanted to make sure she had enough money saved up to move. It seemed like every time she got paid her mother was asking for half of it! How could she survive with only half a paycheck to cover expenses for her daughter, herself, and to save for moving fees?? It seemed impossible!!

What was she to do? Something had to give! It was time for her to go, but how? Then out of nowhere an old friend reached out to her and wanted to help her with whatever she needed at the time. Could this be her prayers getting answered? She wanted to know what the catch was. Clearly he really liked her and would've done anything for her, but he just wanted to hang out with her. He was a really nice guy, so she hung out with him. He eventually expressed his interest in her, but he was not her type at all, so she had to be honest with him. Although she admired his dedication and care for her, she did not want to give him the wrong impression at all! He understood they were just hanging out and would only be friends. Through the course of them hanging they shared a lot of deep things with each other. She was his only friend and his feelings started to grow for her. He eventually could not help himself. He could not suppress his feelings any longer, so his agenda started to change. Every time he was around her, she could feel his energy and it became awkward at times because she just wanted to remain friends with him. At this point she knew she had to become distant because she did not want to hurt his feelings. She had it made up in her mind that she wanted nothing more than his friendship!

He noticed her wanting to spend less time with him, so he constantly thought of ways to try to buy her time and attention at this point. He offered to pay the security deposit for the apartment she was interested in. He knew she needed the money, but she did not want to take it on the basis of them being anything more than just friends. So she had to lay down rules before she accepted the help. He even wanted to pay off all her furniture as well that she had on layaway for her new apartment. She was overly grateful, but continuously reminded him of how much their friendship meant to her. She did not want anything to ruin the friendship even though his desires of wanting more of her grew.

She took him up on his offer! She then was able to move out of her mother's house and into her very own apartment with his help. She could not believe that she achieved this goal on her list!! Of course she hoped for things, but when it finally happened it was almost unbelievable! She was finally out in her own place and it felt great!! She was finally in control of her own future and could not wait to see what was next.

After about six months later, she ran into the guy that held a piece of her heart and had her name signed on his neck. Just one glance at him brought back all the feelings she had for him. It was almost like he had strings connected to her heart that linked to his and she could not escape from him. She did not mind though because her heart skipped a beat every time he smiled at her and she melted every time they touched.

She was in love all over again and so was he. It was kind of sick if you really thought about it. She still did not want to rush anything, so she proposed that they took it slow and just got to know each other more. He agreed. He had some time to think and loved her enough to honor her request this time. She was now excited to see where they would go from there.

Meanwhile, she still had the friend that wanted more from her and trying to win her over. She knew it was time to cut him completely off because he was not trying to just be friends anymore. She was in love with someone else, so she had to sadly end their friendship after trying to preserve it. She felt bad because she really enjoyed hanging out with him and he helped her like no one else ever did! But she had to let him go until he was able to stick to just being friends or else they could not be anything.

She was now a few months into her relationship and everything was going great! Finally she felt like this could work. She felt that this could be the start of her forever with him. She enjoyed seeing him interact with her daughter and having their bonding moments. She started opening up to him more and more each day. She felt everything was going perfectly until he called her upset one night. He had gotten into an argument with his foster mother and she wanted him gone. His foster mother kicked him out of the house and he had no place to go. Of course she did not want to see her boyfriend out on the streets, but she did not feel comfortable enough yet to move him into her place. She felt that this was another situation he had pushed off on her to have them moving too fast!! She loved him and had compassion for his situation, so she allowed him to move in with her under a few conditions.

She told him he had to get a job to help out with half of the bills, help cook and clean, and save money to move into his own apartment. She was not ready to make this transition a permanent move.

One day she could see it, but not right now! Right now everything was just temporary. She reminded him that upon them getting back together she did not want to rush anything and he agreed. He was on board with the conditions and moved in.

A few weeks went by and she noticed he had not even thought about looking for a job! She was not trying to rush him or hover over his neck, but she still wanted to see some type of productivity! He literally woke up every day to eat, play his video game, and went back to sleep. She felt some type of way after seeing this pattern because if he was supposed to be her future husband, he definitely was not giving her anything to look forward to! She worked full time, went to school full time, full time mother, cooked, washed clothes, and cleaned!! She was exhausted on the regular. She basically did everything, even paid all of the bills. She started asking herself, why did she allow this man to move in?? Why is he here? Yes, she loved him, but love is not helping her pay the bills! Love is not helping her around the house either. He was not even cleaning up behind himself and was always eating up all the food! It was like she had an irresponsible roommate or another child living with her. She started to wonder why his foster mother kicked him out of her house. Could it have been because he was lazy and messy? Guess she did not have to wonder anymore because she got the answers just by watching him every day living with her.

A month had passed and still no progress so this had caused her to view him differently. No more did she have that floating on cloud 9 thoughts, but she viewed him as a user! He was freeloading off of her and she had to put her foot down! She gave him an ultimatum. He had to get a job or get out of her place and their relationship would be over! Another month had passed and he finally got a job. She was thankful, but he made up excuses of why he still could not help with the bills. He only had one bill of his own which was his cell phone, and that was not his whole check. He always made her feel like she was asking him for a lot when actually she was not even requiring much from him. She just wanted him to grow up and be the man like he claimed he was! She shouldn't have to tell the man what needs to be done in the home over and over. She shouldn't have to handle all of the responsibilities alone and she has a "man" sleeping right next to her every night!! She was over it and annoyed with everything now.

They started arguing every day and became distant with each other. How could this be and they lived together? She wanted peace and love in her home, but there was none. She felt this feeling before in the past, but she did not want to believe that their relationship was coming to an end. She wanted to have hope and give him the benefit of the doubt, but this feeling would not let up off of her! When it was all said and done the truth started exposing itself!! He was too busy giving his time and attention to another woman! She couldn't believe it and didn't want to believe what she found out!! Again, this town was small so news traveled fast. All the time she spent at work to get the bills paid because she Had to, he was at Her house with another woman. And when she found out he had the other woman in Her bed, the relationship was definitely over! There definitely had to be angles with him that day because he didn't die slowly! All she could think of was the story she was going to tell the police once they discovered his dead body. The only thing stopped her from killing him was the thought of no one there to raise her daughter while she was in jail, if she went! If only she could figure out how Not to go to jail! That was the thanks she got for taking him in??? He used her then had a nerve to be cheating on her too? Why is it that every time she tried to do good, bad things came her way?

The night she found out she lost it and wanted him gone immediately!! He tried to plead with her so he could stay, but she did not want to hear a word he had to say! She started throwing all his belongings over the balcony and they began to fight. This did not phase her because she was use to them physically fighting. She was ready this time. Piece by piece his things went over the balcony onto the ground! He was lucky he didn't go over the balcony too! The cops were called because of all the noise and they ended up escorting him off of the premises. All he had to do was leave when she asked him nicely the first time, but he could not even do that! He wanted to put up a fight knowing he was wrong, so he got what he deserved.

After she calmed down, she could not believe how that situation escalated to that extreme outcome with the police involved. She was officially done with guys and/or relationships for a while and she made up in her mind that no guy would ever live with her again! She did not even want a guy to visit her place! He would have to have his own place and invite her over to his house. She went back to the drawing board in her mind and had to start the process over again. What process was that? You got it, *erase and replace*! She was definitely erasing things, but she held off on a replacement for right now.

Chapter. 7
The Downward Spiral

Weeks had passed and she noticed she missed her period!!! What was going on?? She could not have been pregnant because she didn't even remember the last time they were even intimate! She rushed and took a pregnancy test and it said she was PREGNANT!!!!! Why??? This just couldn't be happening! She was officially done with him and was not going to be that one that's only in the relationship for the baby! Nope! Nor did she want another baby daddy that she had to drop the baby off with!!! He didn't even have a place to stay! She wanted to die right then and there! She was lost on what to do! She didn't even know if she should reveal it to him or not. She just wanted him gone along with every attachment!! She gave it some months to think about it, then she told him. He said he was scared and he felt he was too young to have a baby right now. She wanted to kill him all over again because if he felt "he was too young" why was he playing house in the first place?? So she kindly hung up, changed her number, and set up an appointment to get an abortion. She didn't know what else to do! She was already struggling with one child as a single mother with no help from the father and she surly did not want two on her hands in the same position!

She got the abortion, but was devastated after it was all over. She became so depressed that she was thinking of thoughts of suicide! What just happened? Why did she feel this way? She definitely wanted him gone and now he's gone, so where did these emotions come from? Every feeling that had ever been swept under the rug in her life had All came storming out! The feelings that she bagged up and thought were gone flooded her mind like a tsunami at that very moment. She needed time to process all that had happened, so she shut down from everyone and everything. She began to soul search, but kept coming up blank! She continued with life the best way she could, even though she was hurt and wounded. A couple months went by and she slowly started pulling herself out of the dark place she was in although she wanted to stay there longer.

The thing that helped her to move forward in the process was that her birthday was approaching and she was turning twenty-one years old! She was a little excited to officially be an adult, so she just had to celebrate a little. She was legal to do as she pleased, according to the law. This opened a new chapter in her life and now it was time to focus on exploring new things..

She started hanging out at clubs, bars, you name it. She stared drinking because that was the highlight of the atmosphere, so she had to partake in it or she didn't feel comfortable. She wanted to fit in. After her first night, she enjoyed the feeling of being intoxicated because it erased the cares of the world in her mind for that moment. It was a new way to release stress for her. Drinking put her mind in a relaxed state! So relaxed that she just had to go out again. She found a replacement without even looking for it and it was exciting! So she indulged more and more until she officially replaced her sleep and the thoughts of her ex-love with drinking and partying!!

She partied every other night. She still went to work, school, and cared for her daughter, but she had to make partying a part of her life as well. She could not add any more hours to the day although she wished she could, so something had to be sacrificed. Sleep it was. She partied so much that she didn't even remember what day of the week it was half of the time.

The party life was a whole new world for her. It became an addiction for her. It was everything she thought she needed under one roof. Music, food, men, alcohol, attention, opportunity, and freedom to explore!! No strings, no attachments, nor were there any commitments to be made. And she had tons of options!

Months of partying turned into years. Soon this was just a normal part of her life until the void on the inside of her started to speak again. She did not want to hear anything it had to say, so she partied even more to drown out the sound! It worked for some time, but it just was not as fulfilling as it was when she first started. The attention and opportunity was not as appealing anymore. And the freedom was not as free feeling anymore. She started to feel the opposite of free. She felt as though she was in bondage. A slave to the night life that only drained her out mentally and physically! She began to feel lifeless and life became a routine. She felt as if she was a zombie that was dead inside. She wanted to stop, but did not know how. She thought if she had stopped partying, she would miss another burst of excitement. It was like a drug to her. She thought she would feel that same high she felt in the beginning when she first started. This is why people elevate to a stronger drug because they are chasing the high, not realizing the high will only happen in the beginning of each stage. She allowed loneliness to overtake her so she just couldn't sit home alone. The streets would call her even louder then! Her thoughts sitting at home alone was one day she would be the lonely old lady with all the cats if she didn't find someone! Her biological clock started ticking and she knew if she still wanted to be married one day she had to do it before she turned thirty. After thirty, women are viewed as old to most men and they then turn to the younger women. Therefore, she was forced to rush to get married like most women. Then they end up lowering their standards accepting anything and everything.

Being alone and feeling lonely were two different battles for her. Alone was a physical thing. She would physically sit in her room alone with just silence. No one was there, just her. But loneliness was the feeling she had on the inside that told her the life she was living was not good enough because something was missing! And when she sat alone she felt the loneliness even more!! She could also be in a crowded room full of people and still felt lonely. How could that be? People suppose to bring company, right? When you're looking for something or someone in particular, you will never be happy with a replacement. In so many words, she was settling and did not even realize it.

She was dying for adventure and she thought going out and meeting new people every night at the club would be the answer, but clearly it was not because she still was lonely. Going to the clubs actually became a boring routine for her. She started seeing the same people, hearing the same music, and started to become numb to the effects of the same drinks. She continued to party though with hopes that one day it would change for her.

Suddenly, her father became ill and was admitted into the hospital. Her father had dealt with an illness all his life. So being admitted into the hospital should not have been a surprise, but this time things felt different. They kept him in there for a few months and nothing they did helped him to get better. She could feel it in the pit of her stomach that something was not right, but she could not figure it out! She elevated the amount of partying at this point because she did not want to think of the "what ifs" pertaining to her dad.

This elevation in partying started pouring over into her mother/daughter time. She felt bad because she had always put her daughter over any and everything, but this void and stress of her dad's health started taking over her mind!! She could not concentrate on the simplest things anymore. Something had to give!

After a few months of her dad being in the hospital and test after test, the doctors determined that there was nothing more they could do. Her dad's digestive system shut down. With him having a blood disorder, they could not operate on him so he was left to die. Her mother decided to take him out of the hospital so he could be somewhere comfortable and with the family for his last days. He held on for three days. Then on October 1, 2007 his body passed away and his soul went to be with the Lord.

Chapter. 8
Daddy's Gone

This was a day she could never forget. Daddy's little girl was daddy-less! She could no longer hear his voice, nor could he give her that big hug she needed when she felt like giving up on life. She felt lost and depressed. A part of her died along with her dad that day. Her dad was her safety net. She felt if all else failed she could go to her dad and he would always know just what to do and/or say. What do you do when your safety net is gone and there is no one else to fill the position? Her world stopped and everything disappeared around her. It was as if she was alone in a cold world with no one to turn to! For the first time in her life she felt complete emptiness! She had entered into a very dark place with no hope of recovery. The person she knew had gone away.

So what did she do? She looked for something to fill the emptiness of course. She started to use men to try to replace her dad, but that did not go too well in the beginning because she thought too hard about everything. She needed something to relax her mind, so she started drinking more and more! Alcohol became her best friend and a major part of her life. At this point she drank so much of it on a daily basis that it took her to drink complete bottles just to get intoxicated! She was addicted to drinking her emptiness away now. But we all know drinking was just a cover up and cover ups are never a permanent fix, only temporary.

Her life was a complete mess now! She transformed into someone else. She no longer could look into the mirror and recognize herself! Who was this person that she created?? She partied every night and slept with a different guy every morning, all while being intoxicated on the regular. After a while she loss count of the different men she slept with and barely could remember their names. She became reckless and out of control! Neither could she even remember if they used a condom or not. She even woke up after a few black outs not knowing where she was. She became the promiscuous girl that everyone whispered about. Every man wanted to test her out and every woman hated her because they wanted the attention she got from all of those men. But all attention was not good attention. They labeled her as a "hoe, fast girl, the one that got around, etc..." but that did not stop her from doing the things she did. She did it with no regrets! The only thing that was on her mind was to fill the void and fast no matter how she had to do it.

The alcohol had officially taken over her life. She started slacking off at work by showing up late, and falling asleep there. She even started failing in school and had to take a few classes over, but that did not slow her down at all. She still continued to drink away. The emptiness became so loud that the partying, men, or alcohol could not silence it! She was in over her head and did not know what to do. Her safety net was gone, so there was no one she could turn to.

She had other family and friends, but no one could rescue her from the pit like her dad could have. It was just something about her dad's words of encouragement that made everything all better no matter if she was still in a mess or not. He was her peace in the storm, but her peace was now gone. She started thinking thoughts of suicide because that meant she would not have had to deal with the stress of life anymore. She could also be with her dad again. But looking at her daughter every day would not allow her to complete the action. When she gave birth to her daughter, she made the commitment to give her daughter the best of everything! And if she died, she would be giving up on that commitment. She could not just leave her daughter alone to feel loneliness! She loved her daughter way too much to let her down. Nor did she want her daughter to ever feel the emptiness that she felt inside after her dad died.

She had to get her life in order, but it was hard to even start the process. Distractions started overwhelming her left and right. She still had goals that had to be fulfilled as well. College was a major one so she could finally start the career of her dreams. She desired to make more money so she could work less and be home with her daughter a little more. She slowed down on partying, but was still fighting with the addictions of men and alcohol.

Men were like this drug that she just could not say "No" to. They felt good for the moment, but when the smoke cleared they caused her great pain. She started the cycle of one night stands because she didn't want to commit and when she did think about it, the guy did not qualify. The down fall of hoping from one guy to the next for her was the guys that was trying to trap her to keep her around! They would get her pregnant thinking that would change her mind about staying with them. Before she knew it, she was pregnant by multiple men and making regular appointments at the abortion clinic! She had to go back to "erasing and replacing" more than ever now!! The number of abortions started to climb, so she had to quickly erase them out of her mind, then replacing the pain with more men and alcohol. The men was for company and the alcohol was to suppress the thoughts.

She knew she wanted to get married one day and have more children, but at this rate in and out of the abortion clinic she was surely damaging her body. She was also decreasing her chances to produce more children every time she got the procedure done. She had to give up sleeping with random men for the sake of her health. Not to mention all of the STDs out there that she could've caught as well, but she was slipping through the cracks and coming out clean. She had to value her health and start making better choices so she could be around for her daughter. She was on a quest to find a guy to settle down with now because she knew she did not want to be alone or continue with one night stands. She was still fighting with her voids so she held onto the alcohol and it held onto her!

Chapter. 9
That Night

She started to experience more black outs that disabled her from remembering anything from the night before. She did not realize that she was doing this to her own body with the amount of alcohol she drank per day. Fortunately, she had one more month of college before graduation! Maybe that would help eliminate some stress, so she did not have to drink as much. She really was excited to finally make it to this point in her life despite all the twist and turns.

But she still was not truly happy. She thought she would be able to experience this moment with her dad. It was because of him that she pushed so hard to get through college. She wanted to make him proud! Instead she just had to keep telling herself that he was smiling down from heaven and he was indeed proud of her. Sometimes she believed it and other times she was uncertain.

But regardless of how she felt, she would soon be graduating. She could not wait to check this goal off of her list! Her friends found out she was officially graduating in a week or so and wanted to have a party to celebrate. She had not partied in a while, so she was really looking forward to this! The time had finally come and it was time to party. It felt so good to celebrate with her friends. She partied with a purpose for the first time and it felt wonderful. Although she had to work the next morning, she partied like it was her first time. The party lasted until the break of day and soon she would have to leave for work. Luckily she brought her work clothes along with her so she did not arrive late to work. The party had now come to an end and off to work she went.

She was so exhausted and sleepy all at the same time. She had to fight to stay awake! She was not that far from work and all she kept thinking about was just making it to work and then she would be ok. She would be able to rest for a little when she got there. She started to regret getting intoxicated and then trying to drive right after! But she did this every time she went out to party, so what was so different about this time? Why did she feel this way?? Why did she have to fight sleep so hard this time? Could it have been all of those long nights of drinking that was finally catching up with her.

This drive felt different. She could not seem to find her sense of direction and she felt like she was going in circles for hours! Before she knew it, she blacked out behind the steering wheel!!!!!!!! She did not even realize it. With the car still moving, she regained consciousness but it was too late! She realized she was on the wrong side of the highway going 70 miles per hour!!!! Ahead, she saw a few vehicles, so she tried to figure out something fast as she slowed down. But the vehicles were approaching her even faster! She saw two cars and a huge delivery truck. There was one vehicle in each lane of the three. She then attempted to pull the car on the shoulder of the road only to realize that there was NO shoulder on that part of the highway! What should she do now???

She ran out of options and time. She could not use *erase and replace* to get out of this one. She suddenly seen her life flash before her eyes and all she could think of was her daughter. How did she get to this point? She appeared to have it all under control to the outside world, but inside she was broken and a mess. Why did she have to *erase and replace* so much that it has now erased everything that she worked so hard for and even erased herself in the process? Why did she replace her problems with things that were no good for her? This feeling was not feeling too good to her now. Actually it was the worst feeling ever! Dying without even knowing her purpose in life and leaving a piece of heart behind in a cruel word alone.

One week before graduation and all of her hard work down the drain. What happens with her daughter/ the piece of her heart now? Of course she did not want to leave her daughter behind, but what could she do at this point? She realized at that moment she had much to live for and she just took it all for granted. She no longer wanted to die and the thoughts of suicide left her instantly! She had to live for her daughter if nothing or no one else. The only thing left to do in the last few seconds of her life was to PRAY!

Yes, pray! She knew that there is a God that sits on high and watches over all of us, no matter if we asked Him to or not. He created all and wrote our stories before we were even born. She had no choice but to trust God with this situation at this point. Whatever was in His will/plans for her life would soon be so. She use to talk to God every day when she was younger, but life happened and she forgot all about God. She had not prayed in many years, but she stepped out on faith this night and hoped God would answer her prayers this time like he answered the prayers she prayed for her mother. So she closed her eyes and...

To Be Continued...

Coming Soon

Volume 2
No More Settling
Available MAY/2020!!!!!

available at

www.ingramcontent.com/pod-product-compliance
Lightning Source LLC
Chambersburg PA
CBHW052119070526
44584CB00017B/2555